Copyright © 2025 by Claudeen Martinez

All rights reserved.

No portion of this book may be reproduced in any form without written permission from the publisher or author, except as permitted by Australian copyright law.

Dedicated to my family.
Michael, Sienna, and Gabriel,
who are my earthly Saints.

Long ago in the mountains of Lebanon, there was a tiny village called Bekaa Kafra. It was quiet, peaceful, and full of kindness, faith and small stone homes.

In 1828, a little boy named Youssef Antoun Makhlouf was born. He had dark hair, gentle eyes, and a heart full of love for Jesus.

Youssef grew up with his mother and four brothers. His father died when he was young, but the family stayed strong by praying together everyday.

As a young boy, Youssef would look after the family's cows. He spent a lot of time alone and in prayer. He would sit under trees and talk quietly to Jesus in his heart.

Youssef looked up to his two uncles Augustin and Daniel, who were hermits at the Maronite Monastery of St. Antonios. He wished to live a life like theirs.

Youssef made his own tiny chapel in a cave near his home. He would light candles, sing hymns, and pray. It was his secret place to be with God.

As he grew older, Youssef felt God calling him. He wanted to give his whole life to Jesus and become a monk.

At he age of 23, Youssef left home to follow his dream to become a monk. He trusted God to lead the way.

He joined the Monastery of Our Lady of Mayfouq, and later the Monastery of Saint Maron in Annaya. He prayed, studied, and worked hard.

When he became a monk, Youssef took the name Charbel, after a Christian martyr. It meant he was now living only for God.

Father Charbel worked in the garden, cared for animals, and copied holy books by hand. He smiled quietly and spoke only when needed.

Charbel spent many hours every day praying. His heart was always close to Jesus and he loved the holy Eucharist with all his soul.

Later, Charbel asked to live alone in a hermitage. It was a tiny house on a mountain where he could pray without noise or distraction.

Charbel ate one meal a day, grew vegetables, and slept on the floor. Even the smallest things he did, he did them with love for God.

One snowy night, Charbel became very sick. He went to heaven on Christmas Eve 1898.

After Charbel went to heaven a mysterious bright light shone around his tomb for weeks!

People prayed to Father Charbel and miracles started happening. Sick people were healed, blind people could see, and hearts were filled with peace.

Because of all the miracles Father Charbel performed, Pope Paul VI made him a Saint on October 9, 1977.

People all over the world began to pray to Saint Charbel. From Brazil to Australia, from Lebanon to Canada, his love reached everyone.

Saint Charbel never wanted fame. He only wanted to be close to Jesus. Now people around the world know him as "The Miracle Monk".

Every year, thousands of people visit his hermitage and tomb in Annaya, Lebanon, asking Saint Charbel to pray for them.

Saint Charbel loved everyone - no matter where they were from or what they believed. People from all over the world, of different religions have been helped by his prayers.

There have been over thirty three thousand miracles performed through Saint Charbel to people who pray to him and believe with all their heart in God.

Every year on July 24th the Church celebrates Saint Charbel's feast day. People light candles, pray to him and remember his beautiful life.

Even in today's noisy world, Saint Charbel shows us that we can find God in the quiet, in prayer and in love.

Thank you **Saint Charbel** for showing us how to live a life full of faith, love, and prayer. We are glad to know your story.

Saint Charbel's story never ends because his love lives on in everyone who follows Jesus with joy. Will you be a quiet light for Jesus too?

Dear Saint Charbel,
You loved Jesus
with all your heart.
Please help us be good
and kind, just like you.
We pray that you watch
over us and our families.

www.ingramcontent.com/pod-product-compliance
Lightning Source LLC
Chambersburg PA
CBHW041110070526
44583CB00003B/131